MW01241573

MAKE MONEY WHILE YOU SLEEP

Use the Knowledge You Already Have to
CREATE PASSIVE INCOME FREEDOM
(Go From Idea to Income in Only 30 Days)

MICHELLE KULP

Copyright © 2020 Michelle Kulp

Published by: Monarch Crown Publishing

All Rights Reserved. No part of this book may be reproduced
in any form without permission in writing from the author.
Reviewers may quote brief passages in reviews.

ISBN: 978-1-7354188-0-3

Table of Contents

IF YOU DON'T FIND A WAY TO MAKE MONEY WHILE YOU SLEEP YOU WILL WORK UNTIL YOU DIE

Introduction

Imagine waking up each day with more money in your bank account than when you went to bed. In 30 days, this can be your reality if you capitalize on your existing experience, knowledge, and wisdom to help others.

In December 2019, I started an experiment to see if I could create enough passive income to pay all of my living expenses if I chose not to work.

My plan was twofold. First, write a book a month to generate passive income from Amazon royalties. Second, package all my knowledge into online DIY courses to sell.

I'm happy to tell you that after six months, I earned enough passive income to pay all of my living expenses. I now have the freedom, if I choose, to stop working, take an extended hiatus, or be more selective with my non-passive income services.

My goal is for you to have the same success and peace of mind. When your passive income pays your bills, you choose how to live your life and spend your most precious commodity – time!

By the way, this book is NOT about generating royalties from writing books. I wrote an entire book on that subject — "28 Books to $100K."

This book is about generating passive income by creating an online training course using your unique knowledge and selling it to others who need your help.

In 2005, I started my first online business with my website www.becomea6figurewoman.com. I sold my first online course, "Quit

Your Job and Follow Your Dreams," and made $2,500 in 30 days. I was hooked! I turned that course into an Amazon bestselling book that makes money from royalties while I sleep.

After working as a paralegal for 17 years and trading time for money, earning passive income is exciting and exhilarating! If you're used to working a 9-5 job, I know you'll love making passive income. And, if you're like me, you'll LOVE not having to be in an office.

Transforming your unique knowledge into a signature online program that you can sell repeatedly is the apex of working smart, not hard!

In, this book, I'm going to share everything I've learned while creating multiple streams of passive income — including what's working now and what's not working.

I currently have a multi-6-figure business with my www.bestsellingauthorprogram.com, where I sell a high-ticket done-for-you program; I also sell low-ticket DIY online courses. My online training program for my bestselling author program is not advertised on my website, as it is my "secret" down sell for those who aren't a good fit for my high-ticket program.

Make Money While You Sleep is a step-by-step blueprint that will show you exactly how to use your real-world knowledge, wisdom, and experience (your Intellectual Property) to create a profitable online course that makes money 24/7. Yes, even while you sleep!

Creating an online course gives you a BUSINESS ASSET that will continually generate money for you and your family.

There are many different paths and philosophies on creating and selling online courses – sell high-ticket, sell low-ticket; add coaching, don't add coaching; create it first and then sell it; sell it first and then build it. It can be confusing and overwhelming.

The goal of this book is to teach you my Lean Launch Method (LLM), so you can create your first online course in 30 days or less with easy-to-use online tools.

I know people who spent months, and sometimes years, working on their online program to find out people weren't willing to pay money for it. You can avoid that by "validating before you create," which I'll explain in this book.

Creating an online program is perfect for anyone with a desire and deep commitment to share their valuable expertise and wisdom with others while making large profits.

My Courses (past and present)

- Quit Your Job and Follow Your Dreams
- How to Create a Mission Statement
- How to Start a Profitable Blog
- How to Make Your First $1000 Online
- Creating and Selling Information Products
- Getting in the 6-Figure Game
- Bestseller Biz Academy
- 28 Books to $100K

When you create a **BUSINESS ASSET**, you will have so much more impact, independence and income in your life.

Over the past 15+ years, I've earned income in a variety of ways, such as:

- ✓ Selling Digital Online Courses
- ✓ 1:1 Private coaching
- ✓ Group Coaching
- ✓ Website Design
- ✓ SEO (Search Engine Optimization)

- ✓ Copywriting Services
- ✓ Ghostwriting Services
- ✓ Earning Royalties
- ✓ Done-For-You Services
- ✓ Book Launches
- ✓ And more

And here's what I've learned…

Earning passive income from digital online course sales is the fastest way to leverage your time and create more freedom in your life, especially if:

- You have a full or part-time job
- You are a busy mom or dad
- You are a busy speaker, coach, consultant, or business owner
- You have a full life

According to Forbes[1], the eLearning market is climbing, and could reach $235 billion by 2025. With the lockdowns and social distancing rules due to the COVID-19 pandemic, online learning is where the world is headed, and it's time for YOU to get on board the money train.

Wouldn't you love to tap into and profit from this multi-billion-dollar industry?

You absolutely can, but *first,* I must share with you the four biggest mistakes I see people make when trying to make money selling online courses:

---

[1] https://www.forbes.com/sites/tjmccue/2018/07/31/e-learning-climbing-to-325-billion-by-2025-uf-canvas-absorb-schoology-moodle/#45b4eef13b39

1. **OVER-COMPLICATING.** Spending months or years on activities that don't get money into the bank account, such as creating logos, selecting colors, branding, business plans, unnecessary certifications, endless research, and expensive websites that don't convert. Instead, focus on a few profitable activities to keep it simple. Here's a secret… if you want to *multiply* your income, *simplify* your business. I'm going to teach you the **Lean Launch Method (LLM)** to quickly get cash into your bank account, even without an email list or website.

2. **GOING TOO BROAD.** Making a program too broad, believing *everyone* can benefit from what's being taught. You can't reach everyone. If you want your target market to hear, you have to call out to them. You either *niche and grow rich* OR *go broad and go broke!* Your online course is NOT for everyone, and I am going to help you become crystal clear about who is NOT a target customer for your course.

3. **BELIEVING MORE IS BETTER.** We have an *unconscious addiction* to making things complicated. Don't try to sell a BIG course with dozens of training modules, videos, checklists, and add-ons because, in reality, LESS IS MORE. An online course that contains easily digestible content allows students to take action and implement quickly. I once signed up for a $1700 online course that I never finished because the videos were so long (and boring). It would have taken 4-6 months to go through everything. I recommend creating an online course on a niche subject you have validated that can be completed within 6-8 weeks. Remember, you can always create additional courses for related topics or establish different levels of your signature course once you have your first online course up and running.

4. **USING THE WRONG PLATFORM TO HOST YOUR COURSE**. Not having a way to distribute content prohibits many from turning their knowledge, expertise, and passions into profitable businesses. I suffered from "paralysis by analysis" and spent more than a year researching online course platforms instead of creating and selling my course. Don't let technology stand in the way of your dreams. I will show you exactly how to create your online course so you can make money fast!

If you DREAM about creating an online course, I'm here to tell you your dream can become a reality faster than you think. I am living proof that you can have a successful 6-figure online business that supports your family and allows you to have true time and money freedom.

Once you create a BUSINESS ASSET, you can repurpose the content to create more streams of income. You will become a *Money Magician* once you learn how to multiply and generate your own income streams.

The #1 block to creating an online course is identifying a topic and niche.

I get it.

It's not easy to figure it out by yourself, and you're probably procrastinating because you can't get clear on your topic.

Either you have too many ideas or not enough, and you're *stuck*.

From my experience creating and selling online courses and helping my clients do the same, I know exactly how to select an in-demand and profitable topic that you are passionate about for an online course. I will teach you my 3-pillar method that will jog your memory to find the perfect topic so you can get started.

An online course is merely a means to transfer your knowledge to someone else to help them solve a problem and achieve TRANS-FORMATIONAL RESULTS.

You might be thinking, "Michelle, this sounds great, but I hate sales."

Usually, someone says they don't like sales because they are afraid of self-promotion or have had a bad experience with a pushy or obnoxious salesperson.

Here's a new way for you to look at "sales"...

If you have information that can help someone else, you're doing a disservice by withholding it from others. Any money that exchanges hands represents the value you are providing to your customer.

Also, sales are a transference of conviction, so you must pick a topic that you are passionate and enthusiastic about which will make selling it so much easier.

It sounds simple because it is!

Remember, your brain wants you to over-complicate things so you DON'T TAKE ACTION. If you listen to your "lizard brain" that wants you to keep living in the status quo, you'll never make money online.

Once we select a topic for your online course, we will move on to things like:

- Low-tech platforms to create and host online courses (I've researched many platforms, and I'll show you what I use)
- The Validate and Create method
- Creating a sales page that converts
- Free discovery calls that sell

- Creating Urgency
- Finding your Most Valuable Payers (MVPs)
- Lean Launch 30-Day Blueprint
- And more!

My passion is helping people who feel stuck in a job or career they hate and want to create time and money freedom in their lives by earning passive income.

After reading this book, you will know how to make money while you sleep (and while you're awake).

I've invested more than $100,000 in my education to build my 6-figure online business, and it has paid off in so many ways.

I can't wait to help you create your profitable online course and ***MAKE MONEY WHILE YOU SLEEP!***

Let's get started…

Chapter 1 –
The Profitable
Online Course Trifecta

We each have a unique and extraordinary wisdom that we can share with others to transform their lives. Remember this: People are desperate for transformation, not just information.

A successful digital online course trifecta has these three elements:

1. Your unique wisdom
2. Your tribe (who you want to work with)
3. What your tribe needs that they are willing to pay you for

Trifecta

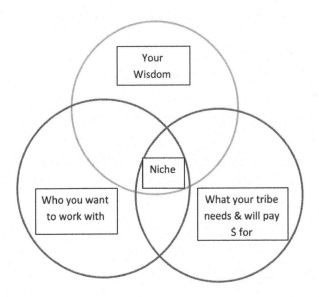

I'm sure you have a lot of ideas about what you want to teach, and that's great.

Or maybe you have ZERO ideas, that's okay too.

In Chapter 2, I share my "Memory Joggers," where I outline my 3-Pillar method to help you get clear on selecting a topic for your online course. I'll also share the mistakes I've made along the way (and have seen others make) so you can avoid making them.

The biggest mistake I see most often is course creators providing what they think customers *need* instead of *want*.

It's important to give your audience what they want and NOT what you think they need.

For example, in my www.BestsellingAuthorProgram.com, I give clients what they want — to become a #1 bestselling author. To do that, they *need*:

- A great title and subtitle for their book
- A unique hook for their book
- An edited and formatted manuscript for their eBook and print book
- A magnetic book description that sells the book
- The right keywords and categories
- A book launch strategy
- A great cover
- Amazon Ads
- Media Interviews

I don't discuss every single detail when I'm signing up a new client; instead, I sell them what they want — #1 bestseller status. Then I give them the components they need to be successful.

Let's look at a few successful online courses in some interesting niches to get your juices flowing:

CASE STUDY #1 – The Social Brand School with Julie and Samantha, who turned $2k in ad spend to $60k with an online course:

Julie and Samantha work with business owners who need help building their brand and offer their students a six-week course for $497 that includes:

- Turning Your Instagram followers into cash flow
- Getting a huge following before you make your first sale
- Getting crystal clear on your brand

Social-Brand-School.Teachable.com/p/SocialBrandSchool

CASE STUDY #2 – The T-Shirt Profit Academy, whose creator made $20k in four months with his online course:

He offers different courses at $179, $279, and $997, and teaches beginners with no design experience:

- How to make six figures selling t-shirts
- How he sold over 34,000 t-shirts
- How to get the same results as he did

TshirtProfitAcademy.com/course/

CASE STUDY #3 - The Virtual Savvy: VA Bootcamp with Abbey Ashley made $41k on her first launch:

Abbey teaches people who want to earn money as a Virtual Assistant to go from start-up to sold out in an at-home business. She often has a waitlist to get into her course.

Abbey teaches newbies how to:

- Work on their terms
- Create a 6-figure at-home business
- Have more freedom
- Get clients
- Package services
- And more

TheVirtualSavvySchool.Teachable.com/p/VA-Bootcamp

CASE STUDY #4 – Lindsay Weirich teaches watercolor painting and launched her first course at $79 and had 246 sales. That's almost $20k!

Lindsey teaches essential tools and techniques for watercolor painting to people who want to learn the art. Some of her topics are:

- Foundations and building blocks
- Tools and supplies
- Techniques
- Painting tutorials

LindsayWeirich.Teachable.com/p/Essential-Tools-
and-Techniques-for-Watercolor-Painting

These course creators have one thing in common—the Trifecta.

When designing your online course, include these three Trifecta elements to ensure you are successful:

1. Your unique wisdom
2. Your tribe (who you want to work)
3. What your tribe needs that they are willing to pay you for

Next, in Chapter 2, we will use my 3-pillar method to explore some ideas for topics to teach in your online course.

Chapter 2 –
The 3-Pillar Method
to Tackle Your Topic

Deciding on a topic for your online course can be challenging. Over the years, I've created more than a dozen online courses, and I either have too many ideas or not enough.

Sound familiar?

Don't worry; I've come up with three pillars that will help you gain clarity about what to teach in your online course. We'll use these three pillars to help jog your memory while exploring potential topics for your online course.

PILLAR ONE: SCARY TIMES SKILLS – Life challenges, struggles, and obstacles that you have overcome can make an excellent topic for your online course.

PILLAR TWO: JOB AUTOPSY – Your skills, talents, and expertise that you enjoy and/or others say you are good at are perfect for an online program.

PILLAR THREE: THE CURIOSITY MAP – Identifying your curiosities and following the bread crumb trail can lead to a great topic for an online course. You are probably an expert at many things, but you just don't realize it!

Don't be concerned that there is too much competition in the area you want to teach. There may be online courses similar to your course, but that usually means there is a high demand for your topic.

Adding your unique story and messaging to a course will distinguish your program from other programs.

Stories are compelling, and if you can tell your story in an authentic, engaging, and persuasive manner, people will connect with you and sign up for your course because they will know you are the real deal. *Your* story, *your* personality and *your* style will make *your* product, program, or service **unique**.

When you love what you teach, others will feel that enthusiasm and excitement and be wildly attracted to you.

Let's do some investigative work that will help you TACKLE YOUR TOPIC for your online course.

PILLAR # 1: SCARY TIMES SKILLS: CHALLENGES, STRUGGLES, AND OBSTACLES

Let's take a deep dive into those scary times in your life and identify what you learned and see how you came out on the other side of these challenges, struggles, and obstacles.

I love having a coach who has overcome a challenge that I am struggling with because they can teach me what they learned while going through that experience.

Life brings us many unique "lessons"; some we label "good" and others we would rather forget. Our hardest lessons can provide an opportunity to teach others what we have learned.

A great example is Chris Wark (www.chrisbeatcancer.com), who was diagnosed with stage 3 colon cancer at age 26 and decided to forgo traditional medical treatment and take a natural and holistic path. He now teaches others to do the same. Chris has a book, online course, podcast, and a passion for helping others diagnosed with cancer. I love what he stands for and what he teaches!

Ask the right questions and you'll get the right answers.

I have some questions to help you remember how you overcame obstacles in your life.

For example, I overcame fears and learned many lessons by leaving a dead-end corporate job that was sucking the life out of me. I worried I would not be able to support my three kids and that I would be broke and struggling. The unknown terrified me. Now that I've left the corporate world and have a successful 6-figure online business, I share what I learned with others and teach them how to start their own successful online business.

I did it, and so can you!

Find a quiet place where you can be alone to contemplate, reflect, and answer the questions below to see if there might be an idea for an online course lurking here.

MEMORY JOGGER #1

What challenges, struggles, or obstacles have you overcome in your life that might position you to help others in a similar situation?

Don't over-complicate this exercise. Just think about PIVOTAL MOMENTS in your life that you could possibly teach others.

Examples: Have you overcome a financial situation, a health crisis, a relationship problem, a spiritual awakening, a career shift, a family challenge, an affair, an abusive relationship, etc.?

Below, list any significant obstacles that you have successfully navigated through and come out on the other side.

_____
_____
_____
_____
_____
_____
_____
_____
_____
_____
_____

MEMORY JOGGER #2

Write 1-10 sentences describing how you overcame these challenges, struggles, or obstacles. What results did you achieve by working through the challenges?

_____

_____

_____

_____

_____

_____

_____

_____

_____

_____

_____

_____

_____

_____

_____

_____

_____

_____

_____

_____

_____

_____

MEMORY JOGGER #3

When you think about a difficult situation, what help or resources do you wish you had to more easily work through the process?

_____

_____

_____

_____

_____

_____

_____

_____

_____

_____

_____

_____

_____

_____

_____

_____

_____

_____

_____

_____

_____

_____

_____

_____

_____

_____

MEMORY JOGGER #4

Describe the pain you felt about the situation. Give as many details and use as many feeling words as you can. Be honest about how bad you felt and your pain level at the time.

_____

_____

_____

_____

_____

_____

_____

_____

_____

_____

_____

_____

_____

_____

_____

_____

_____

_____

_____

_____

_____

_____

_____

_____

_____

MEMORY JOGGER #5

When you reflect on the amount of pain, how much would you have paid to resolve it?

_____

_____

_____

_____

_____

_____

_____

_____

_____

_____

_____

_____

_____

_____

_____

_____

_____

_____

_____

_____

_____

_____

_____

_____

_____

_____

MEMORY JOGGER #6

What skills and knowledge did you acquire during this challenging time?

_____

_____

_____

_____

_____

_____

_____

_____

_____

_____

_____

_____

_____

_____

_____

_____

_____

_____

_____

_____

_____

_____

_____

_____

MEMORY JOGGER #7

How can you use what you learned to help others in a similar situation?

_____
_____
_____
_____
_____
_____
_____
_____
_____
_____
_____
_____
_____
_____
_____
_____
_____
_____
_____
_____
_____
_____
_____
_____
_____
_____
_____

MY ANSWERS

1. What challenges, struggles, or obstacles have you overcome in your life that might position you to help others in a similar situation? **After a 17-year career in the legal field, I was burnt out, drained, and despised my job. I was a single mom with three young children to support and didn't know what else I could do to earn money. I was living paycheck-to-paycheck and desperately wanted to get out of that job.**

2. Write 1-10 sentences describing how you overcame these challenges, struggles, or obstacles. What results did you achieve by working through the challenges? **I was let go from my job which was a blessing in disguise. Consequently, I created multiple streams of income to support myself while I figured things out. After a short time, I took an outside sales job, and, within 18 months, was making six figures working half the time of my corporate job. This gave me the freedom to pursue my passions, which were writing, speaking, and teaching. I started my website and began making money online.**

3. When you think about a difficult situation, what help or resources do you wish you had to more easily work through the process? **I wish I had a mentor to help me figure out what to do after being let go from the law firm. I felt lost and confused most of the time. I would have loved to work with someone who had been where I was and came out the other side being joyfully jobless (and not broke!)**

4. Describe the pain you felt about the situation. Give as many details and use as many feeling words as you can. Be honest about how bad you felt and your pain level at the time. **I felt drained every day I had to go to work. I complained about**

my job and called in sick so often that I thought I would eventually get fired. I felt spiritually and creatively numb and stuck in a place I didn't want to be —JOB PRISON.

5. When you reflect on the amount of pain, how much would you have paid to resolve it? **I would have paid thousands of dollars to someone to wave a magic wand and help me navigate leaving a job I hated and creating a life I loved.**

6. What skills and knowledge did you acquire during this challenging time? **I learned to think outside the career box I had been in for 17 years, and I discovered new and fun ways to make money. I created multiple streams of income and made enough to pay the bills. Then I landed my part-time 6-figure, outside sales job, which gave me even more freedom.**

7. How can you take what you learned and help others in a similar situation? **I created an online course for people who want to change career paths, discover their passion, and make six figures from home.**

PILLAR 2: JOB AUTOPSY

Next, it's time to dig deep into your past work experience by doing a job autopsy. This will allow you to discover the skills, talents, wisdom, and experience you can use to create a successful online course.

Provide the following information for your last 3-5 jobs:

MEMORY JOGGER #1

- Job Title
- Job Tasks
- Task rating on a scale of 1-10. (1 – Hated to 10 – Loved)

Example

Job Title: Paralegal

Tasks:

1. Writing pleadings – 10
2. Legal Research – 10
3. Editing documents – 3
4. Filing – 1
5. Answering the telephone – 1
6. Making copies – 1
7. Interviewing Clients – 10
8. Typing on the computer – 8
9. Going to Court – 10

The goal is to see which tasks you find joy in and then potentially create an online course around this high-passion skillset you have. If you excelled at a specific skill but found no pleasure doing it, you would not want to create a course based on that task.

If you've been working long enough, you have skills that others are willing to pay you to learn.

A great example of someone who took her skills to pay her bills is Lynda Weinman. Lynda was the co-founder of www.lynda.com, which was sold to LinkedIn for $1.5 billion dollars! Lynda Weinman taught different business courses at an affordable price. Check out some of the courses at www.lynda.com/business-training-tutorials/29-0.html.

Now it's time to explore the jobs you've had. For each job, list the job title, job tasks, and rate each task.

JOB 1

Job Title: _____

List all the tasks you performed in this job and rate each one from 1-10 (1 – HATED to 10 – LOVED).

1. _____
2. _____
3. _____
4. _____
5. _____
6. _____
7. _____
8. _____
9. _____
10. _____

JOB 2

Job Title: _____

List all the tasks you performed in this job and rate each one from 1-10 (1 – HATED to 10 – LOVED).

1. _____
2. _____
3. _____
4. _____
5. _____
6. _____
7. _____
8. _____
9. _____
10. _____

JOB 3

Job Title: _____

List all the tasks you performed in this job and rate each one from 1-10
(1 – HATED to 10 – LOVED).

1. _____
2. _____
3. _____
4. _____
5. _____
6. _____
7. _____
8. _____
9. _____
10. _____

JOB 4

Job Title: _____

List all the tasks you performed in this job and rate each one from 1-10
(1 – HATED to 10 – LOVED).

1. _____
2. _____
3. _____
4. _____
5. _____
6. _____
7. _____
8. _____
9. _____
10. _____

JOB 5

Job Title: _____

List all the tasks you performed in this job and rate each one from 1-10 (1 – HATED to 10 – LOVED).

1. _____
2. _____
3. _____
4. _____
5. _____
6. _____
7. _____
8. _____
9. _____
10. _____

NOTE: If you have your own business and don't have a "job," think about what you are asked you to do. If you are successful in your business, others will ask you for help doing the same; this is how many of my online courses and programs were born.

www.BestsellingAuthorProgram.com was created after others saw me publish and launch books on the #1 bestsellers list, and they wanted help doing it for their books.

What aspects of your business do people ask you for help doing?

_____
_____
_____
_____
_____
_____

MEMORY JOGGER #2

Using the information from the job autopsy above, list the tasks you gave a 7 or higher rating. How could you use your current or past work experience to create an online course using these skills?

_____

_____

_____

_____

_____

_____

_____

_____

_____

_____

_____

_____

PILLAR 3: THE CURIOSITY MAP

Next up is another method to help you find a topic for your online course using a breadcrumb trail of your curiosities. Here's what we'll be exploring:

- Podcasts you listen to
- Books you read
- YouTube videos you watch
- Webinars you enjoy
- Magazines you read
- What you talk about in your spare time
- Your hobbies
- Your certifications and extracurricular activities

MEMORY JOGGER #1

Name the last 5-10 books that got you excited. Next to each title, explain why you love it.

_____

_____

_____

_____

_____

_____

_____

_____

_____

_____

_____

MEMORY JOGGER #2

Name the last 5-10 podcasts that got you excited. Next to each one, explain why you love it.

_____

_____

_____

_____

_____

_____

_____

_____

_____

_____

_____

MEMORY JOGGER #3

Name the last 5-10 magazines that got you excited. Next to each one, explain why you love it.

_____

_____

_____

_____

_____

_____

_____

_____

_____

_____

MEMORY JOGGER #4

Do you have an obsession or something you talk about regularly? If so, describe it below:

_____

_____

_____

_____

_____

_____

_____

_____

_____

_____

_____

MEMORY JOGGER #5

Name your favorite 5-10 hobbies and explain why you love it.

_____

_____

_____

_____

_____

_____

_____

_____

_____

_____

_____

_____

MEMORY JOGGER #6

List any certifications you have or extracurricular activities you enjoy.

_____

_____

_____

_____

_____

_____

_____

_____

_____

_____

_____

_____

Great job exploring your life! Now it's time to PUT ALL THE PUZZLE PIECES TOGETHER

Consider your answers from the 3 Pillars above. For each Pillar, select one topic that gets your juices flowing:

PILLAR #1 TOPIC (Obstacles and Struggles)

_____

PILLAR #2 TOPIC (Job Autopsy)

_____

PILLAR #3 TOPIC (Curiosities)

_____

EXTRA:

(If you have a business, what things do others ask you to help them with?)

_____

It's important to find something you are passionate about and, of course, helps others. Please take a few moments to answer the following questions:

1. What topic from the three choices above do you feel most strongly could help others?

   _____

2. In what areas do you feel you are a true expert?

   _____

3. What type of person would benefit the most from working with you? Where are they in their life (probably somewhere

you have been in your past)?

_____

After completing these exercises, you should have some great ideas for potential online course topics. This is huge! Be proud of yourself for exploring, documenting, and observing where your energy and passion flows.

Next, we'll niche down this topic even further to create a magnetic title for your online course.

Sleep on it, meditate on it, or pray about it if you like, and then go with the one you have the most energy around. Of course, we will need to validate your idea before you create it to ensure it's in demand.

The #1 topic for my online course is _____

Chapter 3 –
Niche & Grow Rich
<u>or</u> Go Broad & Go Broke

Most people have what I call "niche aversion." They don't want to pick one audience or group of people to work with, and instead, try to sell to everyone!

Niche averse people have a Fear Of Missing Out (FOMO) and believe money is being left on the table if they exclude anyone from their offer.

GO BROAD & GO BROKE

Before I started my online business, I taught live in-person classes and workshops at adult education centers, community colleges, and my church. I wanted to reach everyone.

I remember teaching a class where 80% of the attendees were women, and 20% were men. When I used analogies or gave them exercises to do, the men often said, "I don't get it." There seemed to be a disconnect.

I realized then that my ideal audience was women, and that's how www.becomea6figurewoman.com was born!

Women spoke the same language as I did (i.e., Men are from Mars, Women are from Venus), and I wasn't "efforting" to get my message across.

Some might say I reduced my audience size by half since I was only focusing on women. When I looked at the statistics for self-help readers and the type of courses I was teaching, I discovered that most readers and customers for my topics were women. That's when I decided to niche down and selected women as my target audience.

It's natural to want to reach as many people as possible with our knowledge, wisdom, and, ultimately, our online courses. In our unfocused minds, we want to reach the masses and make millions.

Know that if you go broad, you will probably go broke.

You are much better off trying to reach a small, targeted group of people than trying to reach the whole world.

When you create your message, you must be able to speak to one specific person about their problems. Your online course should be created to provide a solution for that one specific person.

PICK ONE THING

When I hired my first high-ticket business coach, he looked at my website and said, "Michelle, what are you teaching? You have so many different programs."

I admit I was all over the place selling a little of everything.

My coach helped me choose one area to focus on — my Bestselling Author program. Within 90 days, I went from making $3K to $5K per month to my first $22K month!

I picked a niche because of my absolute love for books, and my tribe, of course, was "authors!" I also discovered there was a need in the marketplace for my done-for-you services. It worked well because I am a writer and a published author, so I was teaching others to do what I was doing.

If you want to make money with your online course, you must pick a niche. You can create more courses on various related topics in the future, but for right now, I want you to select a specific audience to reach.

FROM GENERALIST TO SPECIALIST

Author, Speaker and Course Creator, Steve Scott has written 40+ books and makes $20k+ per month in passive income. When he was struggling to make money online, he promoted several affiliate programs.

In 2012, he started writing and self-publishing books on Amazon in the "make money online" space. He did not have much success at first.

Once he niched down and focused on habits, his income grew exponentially. He started his website, www.developgoodhabits.com/ and multiplied his audience size and income.

Be fully aware that your brain will NOT want to niche down. It's going to tell you to help everyone. Don't listen!

PICKING YOUR NICHE

Let's start picking your niche based on your answers to the questions in Chapter 2.

When considering your online course topic, choose from one of the five big areas listed below:

1. Finances
2. Relationships/Dating
3. Career/Business
4. Health
5. Spirituality

Note: some areas have audiences that have money and are willing to spend it; others – not so much.

When I told my coach I wanted to start teaching in the spiritual space, he said, "Great, I hope you like being broke."

My coach was a broke pastor for many years before starting his online business teaching Facebook ads for coaches, eventually earning seven figures.

Keep in mind when you are selecting your topic that the bigger your potential client's pain, the more money they will pay to solve it.

Which of the five areas above would you like to focus on for your online course? (Make sure the audience you are targeting has money to spend).

Some other things to consider as we go through this process:

1. What do people say you are good at that you also love doing?

2. What are your top three core values? (Examples: truth, self-worth, safety, integrity, dignity, relationships, honesty, respect, kindness, freedom, inner peace, service, trust, love, equality, faith, positive attitude, excellence, justice, hope, nobility, wholeness, joy, humility, honor, charity, simplicity, etc.)

3. What group or tribe do you want to serve, inspire, and impact? (Example: women, men, children, the elderly, animals, people with disabilities, health-challenged people, CEO's, Leaders, Introverts, Extroverts, singles, couples, divorced, Authors, Speakers, etc.)

4. What do you most want to teach and represent in this world?

Now that you've done the work and have more clarity, it's time to pick a working title for your course.

Here are some fill in the blank templates you can use:

- How to get [desired outcome] without [usual problem]
- [Number] Simple Steps to [desired outcome] without [usual problem]
- How to get [desired outcome] in [a short time/without usual problem]

Write the working title of your course below:

_____

Tip: *Use www.surveymonkey.com to create a survey and test multiple title ideas.*

Below are some example course titles to help you select a name for your course.

- How to Make Money While You Sleep
- How to Write a Sales Page
- How to Hire a Virtual Assistant
- How to License your Program
- How to Become a 6-Figure Ghostwriter
- How to Overcome a Bad Divorce
- How to Heal from an Abusive Relationship
- How to Ask for a Raise and Get Paid What You're Worth
- How to Become a Full-Time Writer
- How to be Happily Single

Getting More Clarity

My course _____ (1. Working title) helps _____ (2. Tribe; group you most want to impact and work with) learn how to _____ (3. what you are going to teach specifically) so they can _____ (4. the result they will get; what they will be, do or have after taking your course).

EXAMPLE

My course, *Make Money While You Sleep*, helps *People with Unique Knowledge and Wisdom* learn how to *Earn passive income from home by creating a signature online course (business asset)*, so they can *Have MORE time and money freedom and not be trapped in a job.*

People buy programs to get the RESULTS you are promising.

What is the BIG PROMISE to students who buy your online course?

In my bestselling author program, I promise clients that they will become a #1 bestselling author or their money back guaranteed!

Name your BIG promise here:

_____

Your brain is a trickster; don't listen to it.

As soon as you select one thing to focus on, your brain will come up with a gazillion different ideas for new topics. I believe it's a form of procrastination and self-sabotage.

If you want to be successful, pick a niche, and stick with it. Trust your intuition and take into consideration all the exercises and work you've done.

Let's summarize:

- What group/tribe do you most want to influence and impact?
- What are you going to teach this group, and what result will they get?

- What is the working title of your course?
- What is your **BIG PROMISE**?

If you can teach your material in a specified time frame, consider including that in the title to niche down even further. Adding this additional layer will attract people interested in learning that topic but are short on time.

Include the time frame in your working title:

- How to Make Money While You Sleep *in 30 Days or Less*
- How to Write a Sales Page *in 48 hours*
- How to Hire a Virtual Assistant *in the next 7 days*
- How to License your Program *in 90 days*
- How to Become a 6-figure Ghostwriter *in 12 months or less*

Title Tips

- Use a short (2-3 word) title and add a subtitle (7-10 words) that clarifies and adds context to your title, including the student's transformation, results, and desired future state.
- Add a time frame if it makes sense.
- Limit the title and subtitle to two lines max.
- Research other titles in your genre that you like and create something similar. For example, for teaching others how to create online courses, I found titles like "Courses from Scratch," "Courses that Sell," "Launch Academy," "Scale with Success®." These are short and catchy. What can you come up with?
- Create at least five course titles and do a survey if you can't decide which one to use.

If you want to read a great article on finding titles, check this out www.Psychotactics.com/Create-Book-Names.

Define Your Avatar

Now that we have a working title for your course, let's define your avatar and write a letter to your perfect prospect.

Interview someone who is a good candidate for your course or think about someone you know who would be a good fit and answer the following questions:

- Gender
- Age
- Income
- Education Level
- Family Status
- Experience level with your topic (newbie, intermediate, advanced)
- What type of work do they do?
- Hobbies?
- What kind of books do they read?
- Do they have a spiritual practice?
- Where are they feeling most challenged in their lives right now?
- What keeps them awake at night (related to your topic)?
- What is most important to them right now?
- What are their hopes, dreams, and aspirations?

When you interview someone who would benefit from your course, you will get the exact information you need for your message that you can also use on your sales page and in follow-up email sequences (autoresponders).

Another great exercise to obtain even more clarity is to write a letter to your ideal client.

Exercise: Write a Letter to Your Ideal Client

In the letter, acknowledge the client's problems, pain, and fears, and tell them what solutions your course provides. Speak from the heart and explain why you created your course.

Remember, your course is not meant for everyone.

If you still think everyone can benefit from your course, you need to further narrow your niche.

Think about who would NOT be a good fit for your course.

For example, in my bestselling author program, I do not work with authors who write children's books, romance novels, fiction, or science fiction.

Caitlin Bacher, creator of "Scale with Success®," clearly states on her website who her program is designed to help, and who it is not.

THIS **IS** FOR:	THIS IS **NOT** FOR:
✔ Course creators who want to generate an extra $15k-$40k per month from their online course	• People who have NO CLUE what their course will be about.
✔ Course creators who are tired of living launch to launch and want to create consistent, scalable revenue	• People who secretly like being stuck in business so they can make everyone feel sorry for them.
✔ Course creators who are decisive and ready to take action right NOW to scale their business with success	• People who want to join Scale with Success® just to hang out and chit chat, but have no interest in actually doing the work.
✔ Course creators who actually CARE about their students and love to watch them win	

Now, it's your turn…Three types of people my course is **NOT** for:

1. _____

2. _____

3. _____

Now that you've dug deep, selected your course topic, defined your avatar, written a letter to your ideal prospect, and determined who your course is NOT for…it's time to validate your course idea.

VALIDATE BEFORE YOU CREATE

Validate your idea so you don't waste precious time like so many wanna-preneurs do. Here are four methods to validate your ideas, and I recommend you do each one.

METHOD 1: Find courses similar to what you want to create. Check online platforms like: udemy.com, masterclass.com, Lynda.com, or Google your topic with the words "online course." Write down the title, the length of the course, the cost, and list the main benefits. This is your market research.

METHOD 2: Send an email to your list to share that you have a brand new "BETA" program coming out soon called [Working Title of Course]. Include a link to a landing page where they can sign up to receive more information (more about landing pages below). I use Aweber to collect email addresses for my business (you can use ActiveCampaign, Mailchimp, etc.). You don't need thousands of people to sign up — 25-100 people indicates there is good initial interest.

METHOD 3: Send people from your social media platforms to a landing page to sign up and receive more information about your upcoming program.

METHOD 4: Come up with 4-8 titles around the same topic or niche and create a survey using surveymonkey.com so people can vote on the title. I discovered people loved the title: "*Make Money While You Sleep*" by conducting a survey. I had other good titles, but that got the most votes! Below are the other titles I included in the survey:

1. From Zero to 6 Figures
2. Your First $5k Day
3. 6 Figures in 90 Days
4. Big Money Coach
5. Your First $10k Day
6. Quit Your Job and Create Work You Love
7. Make Money While You Sleep (MMWYS)

Always look to the market (real people) for real answers. Don't try to guess or speculate about what people want. I could have gone in a lot of different directions for this book title, but I asked my audience (my email list), and they gave me the answer I needed.

Make sure the people taking the survey are your ideal clients. One way to do this is to start a private Facebook group about your course topic, and once you have 100-250+ members, survey the group.

Create a landing page so anyone interested in your course topic can sign up to receive more information about your upcoming program. Ideally, you want 25-100+ people to sign up. Fewer sign-ups indicate you may not have a good message/offer/title, or there is not enough interest.

Remember, you must share your BIG PROMISE with your audience when you are validating.

Example

> *Hello,*
>
> *I'm creating a new program called "Make Money While You Sleep," which shows experts how to create and launch an online course in 30 days or less and go from zero to $1000+ using my Lean Launch Method. If you are interested in*

receiving more information about my new program, click the link below to sign up: [LINK]

Thanks so much!

Michelle Kulp

Great job! Don't skip the validation step. You don't want to waste time creating a program that has zero interest.

Landing Page Resources

Most email marketing services like Leadpages, ConvertKit, Aweber, ActiveCampaign, Mailchimp, or GetResponse, include features to create landing pages. Here are a few resources:

- ConvertKit.com/features/landing-pages
- Aweber.com/landing-page-builder.htm
- Mailchimp.com/features/landing-pages/
- GetResponse.com/features/landing-page-creator

I use Aweber for my mailing list and I've used Leadpages for landing pages. Most email services include landing pages so you probably won't need a separate provider.

ClickFunnels is perfect since the entire funnel is set up using their software.

Now that we have a working title for your course, an avatar, a personal letter to your ideal customer, you've identified your course audience, and have validated it, let's start creating the course content.

WARNING: Do not start creating a course until you validate the topic!

In the next chapter, we'll create a course outline and list the main points.

Let's get started…

Chapter 4 –
Online Course
Fill-in-the-Blank Template

"Never try to sell something you're not sold on."

~Dan Sullivan

To me, creating an online course is a lot like writing a book. Over the years, I've developed some great systems and processes for content creation, especially since I decided to write a book a month in 2020.

Here are the six steps I use:

Step 1: Decide on my topic/niche

Step 2: Select my Working Title/Subtitle

Step 3: Mind Dump (write everything related to the topic that you want to teach on using Post-it notes)

Step 4: Group the Post-it notes logically

Step 5: Create an outline using the fill-in-the-blank template

Step 6: Use my Rapid Writing Secrets to add more content

We completed Steps 1 and 2 in the previous chapters. Step 3, the Mind Dump, is a great way to start writing the content for your course. I've tried a lot of different methods, and this one works really well.

MIND DUMP

Get a large poster board or a white board, a pack of Post-it notes, and a pen. Start thinking of everything you want to teach on your selected topic.

Here's an example using a new project I'm working on: *Secret Strategies of Six-Figure Women*:

Usually I have 20-30 Post-it notes – which seems overwhelming at first until you understand the process.

Group your Post-it notes together by topic on your poster board or whiteboard. These will become your Modules and Lessons.

Note: I frequently refer to "modules" and "lessons." A "module" is like a chapter heading in a book. "Lessons" under each module are like the subheadings under each chapter.

Here is how I grouped the topics for *Secret Strategies of Six-Figure Women*:

Review the notes in each group, remove any that are redundant, and reword any that might be unclear. Once you're happy with your groupings, then you will transfer the information to the fill-in-the-blank template shown below.

*TITLE: _____

*WHO YOUR COURSE HELPS: _____

MODULE TITLE	LESSONS	HANDOUTS
MODULE 1:	* * * *	
MODULE 2:	* * * *	
MODULE 3:	* * * *	
MODULE 4:	* * * *	
MODULE 5:	* * * *	
MODULE 6:	* * * *	

CREATE AN OUTLINE USING THE FILL-IN-THE-BLANK TEMPLATE

- Module Name – Theme of that Module Topic
- Lessons – Topics around this theme that you will teach in this module
- Video – Indicate if you will have a video tutorial for this module/lesson
- PDF – Indicate if you will you have PDF handouts for this module/lesson

Outlining the content first makes it easier to create an online course. I've written books without doing an outline first, and I can tell you from experience, it takes twice as long to get done. So save yourself time and do the pre-work.

The Post-it notes from the Mind Dump have been transferred to the course outline template for my new project:

*TITLE: Secret Strategies of Six Figure Women

*WHO YOUR COURSE HELPS: *Women Who Want to Make More and Work Less*

MODULE TITLE	LESSONS	HANDOUTS
MODULE 1: FREEDOM AWAITS	1. Get Off the Financial Ledge 2. Hustle till You Don't Have To 3. The Keys to Break Free From Job Prison 4. Survive, then Thrive 5. Creation vs. Consumption	
MODULE 2: MAKE MONEY AT HOME	1. Virtual Money Machine 2. Pick Your Path 3. Duplicate & Originate 4. Combine to Shine 5. Learn and Teach	

MODULE TITLE	LESSONS	HANDOUTS
MODULE 3: FAST MONEY VS. SLOW MONEY	1. No Free Rides 2. Money Mentor Accelerator 3. The Power of One 4. Find BIG Pain Points 5. High Ticket = High Transformation	
MODULE 4: MAKE MONEY WHILE YOU SLEEP	1. Multiply Your Money 2. All Paths Lead to You 3. Buy Your Income 4. Double Your Money 5. Prepare to Execute	
MODULE 5: SIX FIGURE WOMEN CASE STUDIES	1. Lisa 2. Marisa 3. Jackie 4. Bev	

I made revisions to the lesson names as I entered them into the template.

Now you have a working outline for your course that will save you so much time!

Sell, Then Create

You don't have to create the entire course before you sell it.

In the past, I created one or two lessons then signed people up for my program. I released one lesson every week and created the content as I went along.

Some course creators will make all of the content available at once, but it's not required. "Dripping" the content is a great way to pace your students so they are not overwhelmed.

Others will sell their program and then do live weekly webinars. The webinars are recorded and included in the course for anyone unable to attend live or joined the course after the initial launch. In other words, they don't have any content created when they are making sales.

I signed up for a year-long online course last year, and I'm happy to tell you that I finished it. I believe I was successful because I received a weekly email with a link to a new lesson. I would watch the video and read the handouts right away. I didn't feel overwhelmed since I was digesting bite-sized content weekly instead of consuming the entire course at once (like binge-watching Netflix).

If you create all the content before you sell it, that can work as long as you validated your idea before you created the course. Once my bestselling author done-for-you program was validated, I created an online course for those who were not a good fit for the high-ticket program or could not afford it.

The Lean Launch Method enables you to create and sell your course in the least amount of time. If creating all the content will slow you down, create one or two lessons and focus on sales. Don't get hung up trying to create everything before you sell it. You already have your outline, and once you start making sales, you will be motivated to get the weekly lessons done.

Create your course so it can be completed in 6-8 weeks to avoid customers losing interest.

When creating an online course from a book with more than 6-8 chapters, combine a couple of chapters into one module.

Keep your videos short. People love content they can get through in 10 minutes or less. I see more people consuming my shorter videos than longer content.

RAPID WRITING SECRETS

The last step in creating an online course is to create the lessons. Using PowerPoint or Keynote, list each lesson on one slide with bullet points for the main talking points. Create downloadable PDFs for any templates or worksheets that reinforce the lessons.

Use the template I gave you to provide a quick outline for each module, including the main topic, lessons, and any additional resources such as videos and PDFs. Not every lesson will require videos and PDFs, but you should include some in your course where it makes sense.

Write a short script for each lesson so you stay focused when you're teaching and recording your videos.

Below are some of the *Rapid Writing Secrets* I created for the authors in my Bestselling Author program to write their books that can also be used to create an online course. The goal of the Rapid Writing Secrets is to get the knowledge out of your head and onto the paper. Here they are:

SPEAK YOUR COURSE

Record the lesson and have the recording transcribed. Download the "Rev" app to your smartphone and after recording, you can instantly send it to be transcribed. Also, if you include videos in your courses, you can provide the transcripts as a download.

WRITE THE MODULE SUMMARY FIRST

Many courses write themselves once you start writing, so begin with a module summary to help get the ideas out of your head and on to the paper.

GET OUT OF THE HOUSE AND INTO A FRESH ENVIRONMENT

I always get more writing done when I am away from my house. It's easy to get distracted at home doing chores or talking on the phone. Go to a coffee shop, your local bookstore, or just sit outside; anywhere that you won't be distracted from getting your writing done.

KEEP AN IDEA/BRAINSTORM JOURNAL

As ideas come to you, write them in a journal (let your subconscious write your course for you). Once you decide on the course topic, you'll start getting ideas when you're out walking, showering, drinking a cup of coffee or tea, eating a meal, etc. Usually when we aren't trying to *chase* ideas, they will come to us effortlessly.

TEXT YOUR LESSONS TO YOURSELF OR USE THE NOTES APP

When we text others, we get right to the point. Text your lessons via the "notes" feature on your smartphone so you're not sitting at the computer staring at a blank document. Sometimes, we have to trick our brain to get things done.

WRITE YOUR COURSE WITH BLOCK TIME

We do our best work when we are in a "FLOW" state—when a person is completely absorbed in the activity at hand; also referred to as being "in the zone." Do your highest value work first, early in the day. Set this time aside as your block time, and don't do any activities that can distract you beforehand (email, news, social media, etc.).

****

Now it's time for you to select your favorite Rapid Writing Secrets and start writing your content.

Next, we'll talk about the low-tech set up for your online course.

Chapter 5 –
Low-Tech Set Up

When I started my online business in 2005, there weren't many platforms available to host online courses. Today, there are so many it isn't easy to select one to use.

If you ask 10 different people which platform to use, you'll get 10 different answers. I've researched all the popular platforms and have used several different ones over the years.

I've found that Thinkific is easiest to use. I set up my first online course on Thinkific in seven days. I pay $49 per month to host my course on their platform, and they don't take a percentage of the sales like other platforms do.

I've also hosted courses on my WordPress site using the Wishlist plugin. Websites aren't *set it and forget it* and require a lot of maintenance, updates, etc. So, I prefer using a paid platform that is already set up and is regularly updated and maintained.

Thinkific's monthly fee is minimal for what you're getting. Nothing is FREE, and if you are trying to start or run a business using only free tools, you're not going to be very successful. Invest in yourself and your business to provide a high-quality platform for your students.

I got a lot of complaints from students when I was using Wishlist on my site. Now that I'm using Thinkific, I get a lot of compliments – not just about the course content, but also the ease of use of the platform.

Thinkific is a drag and drop platform that allows you to upload your videos, PDFs, and presentations into your modules and lessons.

You can use any platform that gets the job done in the next 30 days. Pick one platform and stick with it.

THE 3 COMPONENTS OF CREATING AN ONLINE COURSE

1. PowerPoint or Keynote slides

2. Video recordings where you teach the details of each lesson

3. Handouts (optional)

Below is the step-by-step process I used to set up a course in seven days that I sold the very next week.

Step 1: Create PowerPoint or Keynote slides for each Module/ Lesson using the course outline you created earlier. My slides were set up as shown below:

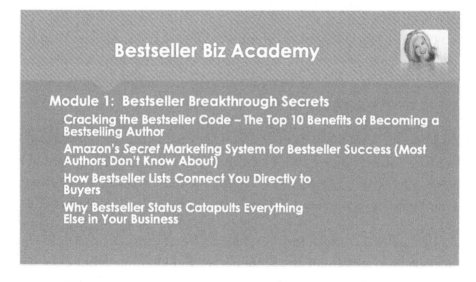

Step 2: Add speaker notes to the bottom of the slides to reference while you are recording your training videos.

Step 3: Pull up the slide for each Module/Lesson and record your video. I use Loom, which is a free service. I've also created videos using Screencast-o-matic and paid services like Zoom, but found Loom to be the easiest to use. I record my screen and then save the .mp4 on my computer. I create a file for each video and keep them in one folder.

Step 4: Set up your course in Thinkific. Add the course name and any course graphics. Then add the Module and Lesson headings.

Step 5: Open each Module/Lesson and drag and drop the corresponding video. If you created a PDF or other handout, drag and drop that file as well.

Step 6: If you have course graphics, you can change the thumbnail for each video so it looks consistent and professional.

Here's what a video thumbnail looks like in Thinkific:

When recording videos, your options are:

1. A screenshare

2. A partial screenshare where you are live in the corner of the video

3. No screenshare. Video recording of you speaking to the camera only

I usually record my videos with option 1 or 2. I use option 3 for my course Welcome video.

NOTE: Thinkific allows you to customize the course settings. Also, the percentage completed is shown to students in the upper left corner of the screen as they move through the course.

I provide a lot of handouts for my students. I create them in Word, insert my course graphic, save it as a PDF, and upload to Thinkific. Below is an example of a handout I created.

Bestseller Checklist
The Foundation of a Great Book!

This goal isn't just to write and publish a fast (mediocre) book; the goal is to put out a high-quality book that will be launched to the bestsellers list and that will stay a bestseller for a long time. With that goal in mind, I have created a Bestseller Checklist for you.

Make sure you have all of these checked off and your book will not only be a bestseller, but will stay a bestseller!

1. START WITH THE END

Pick Your Profit Path Strategy First - The 4 Biggest Authority Profit Engines from a Bestselling Book are: 1) Speaking Engagements; 2) High-Ticket Coaching; 3) Digital Courses; and 4) Live Events. Many Authors are making 6-7 figures on the back-end of their books. Think beyond the book. Your book is just the beginning. It's often the first introduction people have of you and it warms up a cold lead and turns them into a warm lead effortlessly. Once a person reads your book, they often need your help with implementing your material and that's your opportunity to help them as well as to increase your profits from your book. Win/Win!

Thinkific can't make it any easier. If I had my videos and handouts ready, I could set up my entire online course in one day and sell it the next day.

However you set up your course, keep it simple. Don't choose a platform, software, or plugin that requires weeks or months of set up; especially if you can't do it yourself. Pay the $49 a month, and get it set up in less than a week.

Remember, the goal of the Lean Launch Method is to get your course up and running in 30 days. Many people get stuck in the *perpetual planning mode* believing they are making progress, but they're not. They have a "failure to launch" problem, just like the movie. Some planning time is required, but you need to spend most of your time on the execution, or stay broke.

When I was researching platforms to host my online course, I spent weeks watching YouTube videos comparing platform A to platform B, and platform B to platform C, and so on. I became more confused with each option I researched.

Deep inside, we all have either a fear of failure or a fear of success, which keeps us doing everything EXCEPT selling our course. We spend too much time planning and perfecting instead of selling and succeeding.

Don't make this mistake. Allow yourself 30 days to get your course set up, and that's it. The good news is I have the 30-day blueprint all laid out for you at the end of this book!

In the next chapter, we will discuss how to set up a high converting sales page.

I don't have a sales page for my bestselling author course because it is actually a "secret downsell" from my high-ticket done-for-you program. I'll talk more about this later.

My process may be different than yours. I run Facebook ads to an on-demand webinar, and then to a strategy session with me. That's my entire sales funnel and process.

When I get on a call with a prospect, I either sell them into my high-ticket done-for-you program or offer them access to my DIY training course.

I once told my business coach that I wanted to sell my online course directly from Facebook ads. He said "Sure, if you want to go broke, go ahead and do that."

Some people do sell their courses this way, but it's expensive to run Facebook ads, and there is a lot of trial and error involved. Once you get a good ad going, it's challenging to turn cold traffic into a $997 or higher sale. It works better, at least in my experience, to not sell from the webinar but instead to offer a free "strategy session" or "discovery call." This method works really well selling high-ticket since that requires trust, which can be established on the strategy session call.

If you're selling a DIY online course, you need a sales page with a video to create a connection between you and the prospect. You can include a payment button on the sales page or send them to another page to schedule a strategy session with you before purchasing.

I know there are many other ways this can be done; I'm just sharing what has worked for me.

If you have a sales page, make sure you understand copywriting and you have a high-converting sales page, which is the topic of the next chapter.

Chapter 6 –
Ready-To-Go Sales Page

Writing good copy that sells and persuades is both an art and science. If you're an experienced copywriter, you can write the copy for your online course; if not, you can use the fill-in-the-blank sales page below.

Would you like to _____ (state what you are teaching them/benefit) without _____ (problem/what don't they want)?

Answer "Yes," and you'll never have to worry about _____ (problem they have) or _____ (another problem they have) …

Instead, you will _____ (what the outcome will be that they want; the BIG results) and never have to _____ (pain they are in).

You can _____ (paint the picture of what their life will look like when they have achieved the BIG result).

[INSERT YOUR PHOTO or preferably, VIDEO – PEOPLE WANT TO CONNECT WITH A LIVE PERSON]

Dear Friend:

Let's be honest, _____ (what the goal is they want to achieve) is very tough! It's not something can happen overnight, but I can assure you there are some shortcuts. Of course you want _____ (big benefit), but you've tried so many things/products/etc., and they just haven't worked. You just want _____ to stop more than anything else in the world...and you should!

That's where I come in. My name is _____ and my specialty/background is in _____.

Let me ask you a few questions:

Are you _____? (Negative feelings #1 they are experiencing because of this problem).

Do you feel like _____? (Negative feeling #2 they are experiencing because of this problem).

Is it hard to _____? (Negative feeling #3 they are experiencing because of this problem).

Are you tired of _____? (Negative feeling #4 they are experiencing because of this problem).

I know how you feel, because I _____

_____

_____

_____

_____

_____

_____

[THIS IS KEY...YOU MUST ADD YOUR PERSONAL STORY HERE EXPLAINING WHY YOU ARE THE PERSON THAT CAN HELP THEM OVERCOME THEIR PROBLEM. THIS GIVES THEM A PERSONAL CONNECTION WITH YOU AND HELPS THEM UNDERSTAND WHY YOU ARE THE RIGHT PERSON TO HELP THEM].

Now imagine

_____

_____

_____

_____

_____

_____

_____

_____

(Describe in detail here what their life would be like if the problems you listed were solved and no longer existed; create a very detailed picture of how great life will be once they learn what you are going to teach them.)

Sounds too good to be true?

Well, it isn't if you have the right _____
(tools, resources, mentor guiding you, etc.).

That's why I have created _____ (Put
the name and/or title of your course, c.), to help people just
like you _____ (overcome the
problem).

This _____(course) can take years off your trying to
learn this on your own!

At Last! A _____ (describe program in detail that you
have created).

Here's what my amazing, one-of-a-kind program covers (and/or
will help you achieve):

BENEFIT # 1

BENEFIT #2

BENEFIT #3

BENEFIT #4

BENEFIT #5

BENEFIT #6

BENEFIT #7

BENEFIT #8

BENEFIT #9

BENEFIT #10

Sounds great, doesn't it? Well, don't take my word for it, here's what my customers (clients/students) from all over the world (country) are saying about my _____ (program/system/course, etc.):

INSERT TESTIMONIAL HERE. USE PHOTOS IF POSSIBLE AND FULL NAMES. ALSO IF THE PERSON HAS A WEBSITE, INCLUDE THE LINK. (**If you don't have any testimonials yet, offer your eBook or course or product free to three friends or business acquaintances and have them write a testimonial after they've completed it.)

TESTIMONIAL #1 GOES HERE!

TESTIMONIAL #2 GOES HERE!

TESTIMONIAL #3 GOES HERE!

AND IT CAN WORK FOR YOU TOO...
BUT ONLY IF YOU TAKE ACTION!

So, tell me which of these powerful benefits
could help you in your life right now:

Powerful benefit #1

Powerful benefit #2

Powerful benefit #3

Powerful benefit #4

Listen, this may sound like an old cliché,
but if you keep doing the same thing over and over,
you are going to get the same results.

My program (course) is for people who are beyond tired of
_____ (describe problem again) and are
serious about _____ (solution)!

Here are the (3/4/5/6) Biggest Myths about
_____ (the problem/situation)
that will NEVER get you the results you want:

(you must make them believe everything out there and
everything they've tried is not going to ever work)

MYTH #1

MYTH #2

MYTH #3

This is why you need to try something different...NOW!

PROOF POSITIVE

Take a Tiny Glimpse at my Amazing Track Record:

Proof #1 of how this has worked for you or
how you've helped others with this problem.

Proof #2 of how this has worked for you or
how you've helped others with this problem.

Proof #3 of how this has worked for you or
how you've helped others with this problem.

**INCLUDE PHOTOS IF APPROPRIATE.

So you're probably wondering what the cost is for this
incredible resource (product/system, etc.)?

Well, to be honest I know that I could easily sell my product for
_____ (High amount of $/ hundreds or thousands of dollars). I
know without a doubt my _____ (product) has that much value.

But I'm not going to charge you anywhere near that amount because I want this program to be affordable to people everywhere because I know it has the power to change lives!

So your investment for _____is only $_____. Think of it this way...you really can't afford not to "invest" in my program.

In addition to making my product affordable for you, when you purchase my Course NOW, you will receive these 3 Free Bonuses!

FREE _____

FREE _____

FREE _____

Whether you buy my program or not, I can tell you things I know for sure:

The world is not going to change and give you what you want...

People will not change and start handing you what you want...

Your circumstances will not change on their own and start providing what you want...

If you're ready to discover the exact strategies I used (or helped others use) to _____ (describe how this worked for you), and create your own strategy to _____ (describe what they will achieve), then I urge you to (grab your copy of _____) (SECURE YOUR PLACE NOW!)

Click here to reserve your copy NOW!

Sincerely,

***Your name and photo again here.

P.S. Just think...once you complete my program, you'll never suffer through the pain of _____ again!

OPTIONAL GUARANTEES IF ANY

The secret to writing a sales page that converts is using powerful words that are proven to sell.

You can learn more words from the amazing book, *Words that Sell,* by Richard Bayan, and I've listed some powerful words for to use on your sales page.

Powerful Words That Help "Sell" on a Sales Page

PLEASING

1. Satisfying
2. Memorable
3. Unforgettable
4. Special
5. Perfect
6. Entertaining
7. Inviting
8. Appealing
9. Engaging
10. Wonderful

GENUINE

1. Authentic
2. Accept no substitute
3. Pure
4. True
5. True to Life
6. The Real Thing
7. Stood the test of time
8. The one and only
9. Actual
10. Proven/Tested

EASY/CONVENIENT

1. Fast, easy access
2. Accessible
3. Versatile
4. Handy
5. Within your reach

6. Never again will you need to...
7. Eliminates the need for...
8. All in one place
9. Facilitates
10. Simplified

SIMPLE

1. Straight-forward
2. Instant
3. User-Friendly
4. Fast
5. Within minutes (hours/days, etc.)
6. It's that simple...
7. Easy to follow
8. Amazingly Simple
9. Step-by-Step
10. Uncomplicated

EXPERTISE/EXPERIENCED

1. We invented...
2. We developed...
3. Ingenious/ingenuity
4. Trained/Gifted/Seasoned
5. Professional
6. Talented/Talent for
7. Qualified
8. Accomplished
9. Well versed in...
10. Masters at...

HONESTY

1. Truthful
2. Straight talk about...
3. Reliable
4. Factual Information
5. We uncover/unmask/offer proof
6. Sincere/Open/Direct
7. Uninhibited
8. Candid
9. Straight forward
10. Genuine

INSTRUCTIVE

1. Educational
2. Enlightening
3. Unlocks the secrets of...
4. Expands your knowledge/mind...
5. Eye-opening/Mind-opening
6. Illuminating
7. Unique learning experience
8. Answers the questions you've always wanted to know...
9. Keeps you informed...
10. Stirs your imagination...

MONEY-GENERATING

1. Pays off
2. Cash in on...
3. Profit from...
4. Build your Nest Egg...
5. Profitable/Easy Profits
6. Watch your Money Grow
7. Make a bundle on...

8. _____ your way to riches!
9. Double your money...
10. The fast track to wealth...

A BARGAIN

1. Money-Saving Ideas/Opportunity
2. Pays for itself
3. Tremendous Savings
4. Low Cost
5. Fits your Budget
6. The best deal in town
7. Finally, a _____ you can afford.
8. You get more for your dollar.
9. Affordable/Surprisingly Affordable
10. Our loss is your gain.

FAMOUS

1. Favorite/All-time Favorite
2. Acclaimed
3. Celebrated
4. Legendary
5. Endorsed by.../Approved by.../Recommended by...
6. Famed/Famous
7. Always in Demand
8. The People's Choice
9. Known far and wide
10. Phenomenally Successful

ADVANCED

1. Innovative
2. The latest
3. Sophisticated

4. Revolutionary
5. Groundbreaking
6. High-tech
7. Futuristic
8. Unprecedented...
9. A revolution in...
10. A radical approach in...

POWERFUL

1. Mighty/Dynamic/Potent
2. Overwhelming
3. Explosive/Electrifying
4. Mesmerizing
5. Riveting
6. Commanding/Compelling
7. Shocking/Stunning
8. High Voltage
9. Mind Blowing
10. Forceful

PERFORMANCE/RESULTS

1. Fast results/Instant results/Remarkable results/Proven results
2. Increases/Boosts
3. Acts/Performs
4. Works Wonders
5. Works Immediately
6. Gets the job done/Does the trick
7. Raises/Restores/Revitalizes
8. Fixes
9. Pays off
10. Produces/Delivers/Improves

RELIABLE

1. Trusted.
2. Solid/Sound/Valid
3. Proven techniques
4. Carefully tested
5. High performance
6. High standards
7. Top credentials
8. Functional
9. Will never let you down.
10. The quality you've come to expect.

PEACE OF MIND

1. For your protection...
2. Total security/privacy
3. Relax!
4. Takes care of itself
5. You can rely on...
6. Protects your...
7. We're always there when you need us...
8. Your guarantee of...
9. Your assurance of...
10. Safe

SERVICE

1. Guides you every step of the way
2. We do it all for you
3. The solution to your...
4. Solves/assists/performs
5. Prompt Service
6. Helps you...
7. Permits you to...

8. Sound advice on....
9. The answer to all your needs on...
10. We make it easier for you to....

BETTER

1. First-class
2. First-rate
3. Brilliant/Excellent/Elite
4. Unsurpassed
5. Top of the line
6. Unparalleled
7. Nobody beats...
8. Matchless
9. Incomparable
10. Paramount

UNIQUE

1. Rare/Remarkable
2. One of a kind
3. A fresh approach to...
4. Refreshingly different and unique...
5. Out of the ordinary
6. There's nothing quite like it.
7. No other _____ comes close.
8. Off the beaten track
9. Original
10. Hard to find.

FLATTERY TO THE READER

1. We know that you...
2. For people with high standards...
3. You're very selective when it comes to...

4. You're the kind of person who...
5. For special people of your caliber...
6. For those with discerning taste...
7. For those who strive for excellence...
8. You demand the best.
9. For leaders/achievers/doers
10. For those who appreciate only the finest...

ORDERING INFORMATION

1. To grab your copy now just...
2. Your order will be filled promptly.
3. Rush me...
4. Yes, I want to learn about...
5. Yes, I want to enjoy...
6. Yes, please enroll me...
7. Yes, I'm ready to...
8. To sign up and get instant free access, just click here...
9. Don't hesitate...order now!
10. Order now!

DISCOUNT

1. Substantial Savings
2. Price Break
3. Extra Savings
4. For a limited time only!
5. Now only ____.
6. Check the Savings.
7. A steal at these prices.
8. New low price.
9. Take an extra __% off...
10. Don't pay more.

MAKING A DECISION

1. It's a winning decision
2. See for yourself
3. Act Now!
4. Don't Delay!
5. Don't miss this opportunity!/Don't miss out!
6. Now is the best time...
7. Do it today!
8. Put our ideas to work!
9. Order now while there's still time
10. Take this important first step...

THE ART OF PERSUADING

1. This is a once in a lifetime opportunity...
2. The opportunity you've been waiting for.
3. We're ready to prove everything we claim.
4. You won't be disappointed.
5. You can't lose.
6. Why settle for ___, when you can have _____.
7. What have you got to lose?
8. You'll be glad you did.
9. Remember, time is running out.
10. You'll wonder how you ever managed without...

TIME

1. It's finally here.
2. Just in time for...
3. Isn't it time...
4. Long-needed
5. Long overdue
6. Long awaited
7. Just when you need it most

8. It was only a matter of time
9. There's never been a better time.
10. There's no time like the present.

IMPROVEMENT

1. Awakens your creativity
2. Awakens your spirit
3. Your chance to...
4. We'll stretch your mind.
5. Live your dreams.
6. You've dreamed about it, now you can...
7. A golden opportunity.
8. You owe it to yourself to...
9. Gives you the competitive edge.
10. Keeps you ahead of the game.

I can't make it any easier for you than giving you a fill-in-the-blank sales page and power words that you can add to it.

Once you are clear on the benefits your course provides and the problem you solve for others, you will have no problem writing a sales page that sells.

Of course, you could hire a copywriter, but good copywriters aren't cheap. Using the template above is a great way to get started.

Adding a personal video to the sales page is also another great idea. If you are available to do calls and answer questions from your sales page, you will probably sell more courses.

In the next chapter, we will discuss how to determine a price for your online course.

Chapter 7 –
Selling High-Ticket
vs. Low-Ticket

Your goal is to make money. My goal is to show you the pros and cons of selling high vs. selling low so you can choose which path to take. Let's get started.

High-Ticket Pros

- Selling a "course" with weekly Q&A calls has a higher perceived value than selling a DIY course, so you can charge $3k-$10k+.
- You only need 1-3 customers per month to make six figures, depending on your price point.
- You can quickly convert cold traffic from Facebook ads into high-ticket clients with an automated webinar funnel.
- You don't need quantity, just quality.

High-Ticket Cons

- You cannot sell from a sales page.
- You must have a proven offer that gets big results or it won't work.
- You must be good at sales and selling over the phone.
- You must have paid traffic or a very engaged email list and/or social media following.
- It is harder to sell high-ticket only because not everyone can afford the price point.

- Technically, you can't make high-ticket sales while you sleep since you must speak directly with potential clients. Also, one-on-one coaching will require more of your time.

Low-Ticket Pros

- You can sell from a sales page.
- Customers won't have to "think about it" at a lower price point.
- You can make money while you sleep since sales can come in anytime, day or night.
- You can sell from a Facebook group without running ads.

Low-Ticket Cons

- You need a lot of paid traffic to get to six figures.
- You need good SEO on your website to get organic traffic.
- It's hard to sell a course from cold traffic with Facebook ads, and it's very expensive.
- It's harder to make six figures with only one low-ticket course.

I'm not going to tell you to do high-ticket or low-ticket because I don't know where you are on your *make money online journey*. Perhaps you already have a high-ticket coaching program and want more passive income. Maybe you are a newbie and don't have a website, an email list, or a large social media following. You may have made some money online selling services, but want more passive income.

When I started my online business in 2005, I didn't know what I was doing, and I took the path of least resistance, which was to sell low-ticket courses. The first month, I made $2500 selling a $197 course to an email list I built doing live workshops. However, I never made six figures from selling low-ticket courses only.

I've also offered copywriting, ghostwriting, website design, and other services, which are all very labor-intensive ways to make money.

I like to tell people that I am ambitiously lazy. I don't want to work *that* hard, especially the older I get.

I think we can learn something about pricing strategies from Elon Musk. I want to share with you the Tesla 10-year plan and why Elon Musk chose high-ticket first…

In 1996, Elon Musk was making the first "Master Plan" for his business.

Step 1 – create a low-volume, high-ticket car.

Step 2 – use the money made in Step 1 to develop a medium-volume car at a lower price point.

Step 3 – create the highest volume car at the lowest price point.

He did this to make the most amount of money with the lowest volume in Step 1 to fund Step 2 and Step 3.

So, Elon Musk chose to do high-ticket first to fund low-ticket later. You can read the full article here: https://www.tesla.com/blog/master-plan-part-deux

To me, this makes sense. It's hard to build a 6- or 7-figure business with a $97 or $197 product, especially if you are a newbie and don't understand how to generate traffic and convert it into sales.

If your goal is to make six figures right away, use this 5-step automated selling process:

1. Facebook Ad (Instagram Ad/ Linked In Ad) to Cold Traffic goes to Opt-In (Landing Page)

2. Automated Webinar Training (Stealth or ClickFunnels)
3. Call Booking Page > Scheduler
4. Indoctrination Page
5. Sales Enrollment Call

My business coach and I used this 5-step automated selling system for my bestselling author program. Once my offer was converting, we started running Facebook ads, which involved testing the image, the copy above the image, and the call to action (CTA) below the image.

Below are more details about using this strategy.

Success with Facebook ads is all about data and testing. We selected the winning ad once we tested the image, headline, and CTA for 3-5 days at $10 a day.

We were looking for a:

- Click-through rate of 1% of more
- Relevancy Score – 3 or more
- Frequency – Under 2

Anyone who clicked on an ad was redirected to a Landing Page:

Exclusive Webinar On How to Be a #1 Bestselling Author

If you don't have an automated webinar, you can use a lead magnet and run ads. I did this for a year before my webinar was set up.

Lead Magnet with Ads instead of Webinar

I didn't sell a product on the webinar; I sold a FREE strategy session with me. Prospects were required to complete a strategy session application to book a call with me.

You can view my application at: www.bestsellerchat.com or http://bestsellingauthorprogram.com/coaching/

Apply NOW For Your Bestseller Strategy Session with me and
let's talk about it!

Fill out the questionnaire below and after you hit submit, you'll be redirected to my
scheduling software where you can book your FREE Call with me!

***NOTE: My expertise and focus is on Non Fiction Books. I do NOT take Fiction, Children's, Poetry
or Erotica.

Name *

First   Last

Email *

Phone *

Please write what country you are from: *

Business Website - If you don't have one, please type "No Site" *

Is your book published? If so, please provide a link below to your book. If your book is NOT
published, please provide the working title for your book, the idea behind it and why you
want to write this book. *

Please check which one most resembles where you are with your book: *

○ I have an idea for a book, but I need help with mapping it out

○ I know I need a book to help my business, but I'm not sure what book to write

○ My book is written and I need help with publishing and marketing it

○ My book is written and published, I need help with marketing and promotion

○ I have an idea for a book and need a ghostwriter to write it for me and also help
  with marketing and promoting it

Briefly describe your current business: Who do you serve; What do you sell; What's the
price point? *

Why do you want to be a #1 Bestselling Author (Impact, Legacy, Leads, Income, Media,
Credibility, etc.): *

I use Once Hub for Scheduling

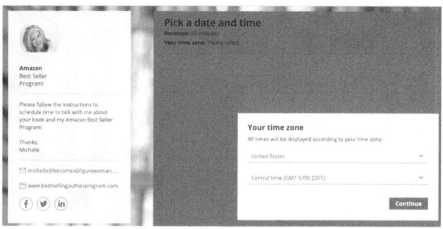

https://go.oncehub.com/BestsellerProgram

*Setting Up Your Indoctrination Page

Your potential client will be redirected to an Indoctrination page AFTER booking a call with you. This page should be designed to create a bond with customers who have booked a call and create a relationship with them.

Record a 15-minute video that tells your story! Don't talk about how awesome you are... NO ONE cares about your awesomeness at this point. If they booked a call, they already are confident that you are good at what you do and they believe you can help them.

In your video, tell your story like you are having a conversation with someone you want to get to know. Highlight the challenges you have overcome that relate to what you help your clients overcome.

Include things like testimonials (if you have them) and extra training you think will influence your potential client to work with you.

If you don't have any testimonials, don't worry. The primary goal of this page is to create a bond with visitors.

I built my 6-figure business using this model. My business requires a lot of my time, and that's why I've been focusing on creating business assets, like online courses, that generate passive income to free up my time.

Three ways I am currently earning passive income:

1. Royalties from my books – I currently earn $2000 per month in passive income from my books; the numbers are growing exponentially each day.

2. Secret down sell – When I do strategy sessions for my bestselling author program, if the prospect isn't a good fit, or

they can't afford the high-ticket program, I sell them my online training at a lower price point.

3. 28 Books to $100K – I created a Facebook group and sell an online course to members with multiple price points.

I plan to add more passive income streams so I am earning multiple six figures just from passive income alone.

So, whatever path you choose, commit to it and go all in.

If you do low-ticket to start, that's fine, because making money with a side-hustle is a great way to get your feet wet and to gain experience.

To do high-ticket, you must already have a proven offer that converts. Never run Facebook ads until you have made money with your offer, or you are just throwing money away.

Next up, we are going to look at how to find your MVP's — Most Valuable PAYERS!

Chapter 8 –
Finding Your MVPs
– Most Valuable Payers

In the previous chapter, I gave you the five steps to run paid ads to enroll clients in a high-ticket program. If you are selling low-ticket, or don't have a big budget for marketing, there are ten ways to get organic traffic.

10 Ways to Get Clients Now Through Organic Traffic

1. **Create a lead magnet** related to your new course that can be consumed in five minutes or less.

2. **Optimize all of your social media profiles** (Facebook, LinkedIn, Instagram, etc.) – Have a public group related to your new program/opportunity.

   a. Create a free Facebook group – use Canva to create a group banner

   b. Post on your personal profile and in your free group

   c. Purchase a domain name on godaddy.com and redirect it to your free Facebook group (it's easier to share and the URLs are typically shorter)

   d. Intro – ADD your domain here (limited space). I help _____ with _____ without _____ by _____.

   e. Fill in Bio information and add your domain to "work and education" add social handles, etc. If you have a Facebook business page, add it to your bio; add photos for your "featured" photos, including some professional photos.

    f.   Balance personal and business

3. **Social Media Posts in Other Groups – Hidden Carrot -** Give really specific advice and mention the overall results you have achieved while being humble. *Make sure you reply to comments and keep open loops going. Take a stand. Get people's attention, but don't ask members to DM you. If they like what you say, they will seek you out.

4. **Social Media Post – Polarity Post (outside and your audience)** – works the best. Think of a hot topic that people will argue about if you mention it. The goal is to initiate intelligent dialogue on a topic* and tie it to your business. Ask others what their thoughts are and monitor engagement. (*NOT religion or politics.)

5. **Social Media Post—New Member Bait.** Once a week, create a post and tag all NEW members. Welcome them to the group, encourage them to introduce themselves, and ask them what they hope to learn or what problems they are having. Finally, remind them to get your FREE Resource (lead magnet) if they haven't already and drop a link to your webinar. (Welcome New Member Script: GROUP NAME is a community of WHO where NICHE learn how to DESIRE. In this group, you'll learn from YOUR NAME, who has achieved INSERT ACHIEVEMENT. **RULES: Do Participate. Do not share promo posts, or be rude to other members. If you haven't yet, grab our FREE Cheat Sheet on NICHE by clicking here: LINK. Finally, please introduce yourself and share what you are struggling with so we can create more content just for you.**

6. **Social Media Post— Test your concepts.** Write an outline for your webinar, new opportunity, concepts, epiphany story, etc. Make an announcement in your group that tomorrow at ** a.m./p.m., you will be going LIVE to cover _____. Go live the next day, and ask for feedback. Try to overcome objections during the live call and see the response. Doing this helps you clarify your message and concepts. Goal: See if your concept resonates with your audience

7. **Social Media Post— Live Q&A.** Schedule a Live Q&A. Prepare stories and responses for possible questions and objections. Watch the live replay and jot down the questions that you covered.

8. **Social Media Post— Post Testimonials.** Screenshot posts from students in your private group OR ask students who had success to record a short video (1-3 minutes) to share their recent success. Ask them to post their success in your private student Facebook group so you can take a screenshot and post it on your personal profile, biz page, IG, etc. Respond to questions and comments. DM directly to take conversation to private messaging. Invite them to a call/strategy session with you.

9. **Social Media Post— Hook/Story/Offer or Hook/Value/Offer.** Grab audience attention (pattern interrupt/hook), then tell your personal story or a piece of your story. Make an offer. Book a call. Explore working together in your program. Give a CTA. Link in comments.

10. **Offer your new webinar to your email list and social media groups as well as to others email lists and social media groups. Incentivize them.**

I signed up clients for my low-ticket online courses years ago by doing live workshops and writing targeted blog posts using keywords. This is known as SEO – search engine optimization.

This is a slower path, but it's FREE! Don't underestimate the power of blogging. I still get clients for my high-ticket programs who found me from blog posts I wrote a long time ago. If you use SEO and know which keywords people are searching for to find a program like the one you offer, it's a great way to generate free traffic.

Many experts encourage selling only high-ticket, but this isn't a one size fits all business.

Customize it to what works for you. How much time you can devote to this endeavor and how much money you want to invest to make it happen will be the two factors that influence your decision.

When I first set up Facebook ads to my automated webinar, some of the costs I incurred were:

1. Automated Webinar software/platform – $67 per month (Stealth)

2. Leadpages – $50 per month ("opt in" to sign up for the webinar)

3. Online training portal hosting – $49 per month (course content delivery)

4. Facebook ads – $700 to $1000 per month *I know experts who spend much more than this. My program doesn't need quantity; I only need 3-4 quality clients per month.

Once you get your Facebook ads running, you can retarget people and customize audiences.

I'm in the process of creating a new webinar and plan to use ClickFunnels to deliver it "on-demand." It will cost me $97 per month, but having an on-demand webinar allows those who sign up to view it right away.

Facebook ads are not easy and I recommend you engage a coach or an expert to help you. Do not hire an "agency" to do your ads because most of them are either too expensive or won't get you the results they promise and will take your money anyway.

If you are going to do Facebook ads with an automated webinar funnel, learn how to do this yourself first. You must understand the process before you try to outsource it.

I believe I've been successful online because I never outsource anything until I fully understand how to do it myself. I invested a lot of time and energy learning many platforms, and it has paid off.

How can you outsource Facebook ads if you don't understand the platform, the terminology, and how it works? You will likely get ripped off. Trust me, I know. I hired an agency once, and they failed big time. Luckily for me, there was a money-back guarantee if a certain click-through rate wasn't achieved. I got my money back, but only after a big fight. They thought I didn't understand the numbers, but they were wrong. Someone without the knowledge and experience from running their own ads would have lost thousands of dollars. Always learn the platforms before you consider outsourcing!

When deciding whether to do low-ticket or high-ticket, here's my recommendation:

If you need to leverage your time, you need income from sources that don't require your time, which can be accomplished through low-ticket DIY online courses.

If you need to generate money quickly and you are trying to earn a full-time income online, start with high-ticket sales and then add DIY online courses down the road.

Next up is how to get sales and create urgency.

Chapter 9 –
Getting Sales and
Creating Urgency

There are multiple ways to get sales for your course. Think about driving somewhere for a vacation. If you use a driving app, you will be given multiple routes to drive to your destination. The same is true for getting sales for your course – you want to have multiple paths that lead to your course.

Once your course is set up, there are multiple ways you can sell it:

- Do a 5-day free challenge in a Facebook group; then offer it with a discount.
- Offer FREE tools or FREE access to a module or lesson. A percentage of people who take the free module will sign up for the paid course.
- Do a live webinar about your topic and offer a discount to anyone who signs up while on the call.
- Blog about your topic using targeted keywords and promote your blog posts to all of your social media platforms and your email list.
- Speak about your topic on virtual summits or workshops, and offer a special promotion to anyone who signs up by a certain date.
- Do daily Facebook live trainings and invite viewers into your program during the training.

- Find an affiliate with a big email list and social media following and offer them a share of the sales to promote your webinar.
- Create a BETA course and offer the first "x" amount of customers a discount for founding members.

I want to share a case study from one of my very successful clients who built a multiple six-figure business around her book by selling online courses and coaching programs.

CASE STUDY

Lisa Phillips teaches beginning real estate investors how to invest in $30-$50k properties in working class neighborhoods. She offers a free mini-course on Thinkific. This is a good strategy because prospects who go to her Thinkific site also see her other available programs at different price points:

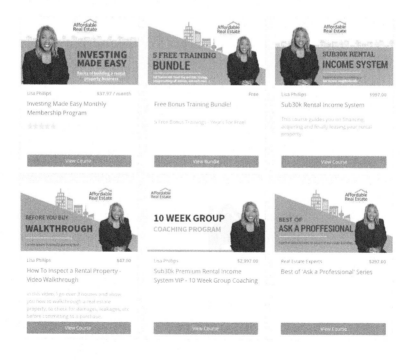

Check out Lisa's free course at https://lisa-phillips.thinkific.com/

In addition to giving away free modules/lessons, Thinkific also allows you to drip feed content so you can offer payment plans and only release content once the payment is received.

Lisa's a brilliant marketer who has mastered combining low-ticket and high-ticket to create a multiple six-figure business!

Next up is my client, Daniel Rondberg...

CASE STUDY

Daniel signed up for my high-ticket bestselling author program to get his book written and launched to the #1 bestsellers list. Five days after we launched his book, he sold a $997 online course and made $23,000 in a one-hour "live" webinar.

How did he do this?

Using someone else's platform and email list!

If you are starting from scratch – you have no list or only a small email list and social media following – this is a good strategy.

Find someone who complements what you teach (not the same as what you teach) and offer them a share of your sales in exchange for promoting your live or automated webinar to their list.

In this case, Daniel knew the author who had a big following, so he offered him 20% of the sales to promote his webinar.

I advised Daniel to sell the course for $997 (he was going to do it for less) and offer a discount to anyone who bought while they were on the webinar. He also added some pretty big bonuses to incentivize the attendees.

Over 500 people signed up for the webinar, and 70 people attended live. Daniel made $23,000 and his partner made $4,600 from offering it to his list and social media followers.

Don't think because you are just beginning that you can't make money fast. Daniel made $23,000 within 30 days of creating his online course. I coached Daniel on how to set up a course, and gave him the webinar slides template, but he took massive action and made it happen.

Be an action taker like Daniel!

When you offer a BETA program, frame it as you are looking for "Founding Members" to join and give you feedback. For example, you can list the price of the program at $1997, but then offer a substantial discount to the founding members.

When I started selling online courses in 2005, it was easier to sell from a sales page and much less competitive than it is now.

I have had the most success selling high-ticket with my 5-step automated selling system, and then offering a secret down sell to my stand-alone online training.

You may be looking to make a few hundred or a thousand dollars per month from a side hustle, and selling a DIY course is a great way to do that.

People will pay high-ticket prices when they want coaching and accountability.

Danielle Leslie is a very successful online course creator. She sells a $1997 course with group coaching, and has taken her business to $10 million using that model. She has mastered Facebook ads, the automated webinar and selling system, as well as follow-up emails and retargeting.

You can check her out at: https://www.danielleleslie.com/

Sign up for her email list and see what she's doing.

Obviously, she didn't do this overnight, and I'm certain she had a great business coach or mentor to help her achieve this massive success. She also spends thousands of dollars per months on paid ads.

Don't compare yourself to Daniel, Danielle, me, or anyone else. Everyone has to start where they are and learn how to be a course creator, online marketer, and entrepreneur.

I promise when your first sale comes in, you'll be hooked and will gain loads of confidence knowing that all your work and effort is finally paying off.

Let's talk about some ways to create more urgency to get people to sign up for your program.

Add value and sell your course by offering bonuses, such as:

- A coaching call with you AFTER completing the course, which encourages the client to complete the course to talk with you. In Thinkific, you can see if a student completes all the content.

- Office Hours that you offer for Q&A to students. You want your students to be successful, and they will have a higher chance of success with your help. Obviously, you don't want this to be a big time suck, so you can offer office hours anywhere from once a week to once a month, or even bi-monthly. Include this a bonus when they sign up and have time blocked on your schedule to allow customers to sign up for a meeting during your office hours. You can set it up on Zoom as a recurring meeting.

- If you have written a book or you have other printed support material, give a FREE copy to anyone that signs up for your course.

Bonuses move people to take action. Offer something with real value, but don't give too many bonuses where they feel overwhelmed. Create urgency by only offering the bonus for a short period of time.

In the next chapter, I share the 30-day blueprint I created so you can get your online course up and running as fast as possible.

Since I started writing a book a month in January 2020, I've learned that when you have timelines, deadlines, and accountability, you can get a lot done in a short period of time.

If you want to be successful, commit to getting your course done and making your first sale in the next 30 days.

Let's get started with your 30-day plan now…

Chapter 10 – The 30-Day Lean Launch Blueprint

I can write and publish a 100-125 page book every 30 days, so I know you can create and launch an online course in 30 days or less using my Lean Launch method.

Warning: Your lizard brain will give you 101 reasons why you can't and shouldn't do this.

My top 10 reasons why you should create and sell your online course in the next 30 days

1. You don't learn until you launch.

2. You can sell an online course *before* you create the content.

3. A minimum viable product is better than NO product.

4. "People don't know what they want until you show it to them." – Steve Jobs

5. Execution matters more than ideas; ideas are a dime a dozen.

6. You won't waste time (weeks, months, years) getting ready to launch or researching your topic; you will spend all of your time on execution and selling your program.

7. When you have a clear end date, it drives you forward.

8. It forces you to focus on paying customers instead of on the myriad of distractions that entrepreneurs typically focus.

9. The technology available today allows you to create and launch quickly.

10. A good plan executed poorly now is better than a perfect plan never executed.

There is no reason you can't create and sell an online course in 30 days. If you don't get paying customers, you may be a wanna-preneur and not an entrepreneur.

Execution is all that matters.

30-Day Blueprint to Create, Validate and Sell Your Signature Online Course

Day 1: Choose your topic for your online course using the 3 pillars: Scary Time Skills; Job Autopsy and the Curiosity Map.

Day 2: Select one of the 5 Big Areas to focus on: Finances; Relationships, Career/Business, Health, Spirituality. Make sure your target audience has money to spend.

Day 3: Answer these 4 questions: 1) What do people say you are good at that you also love doing? 2) What are your top three core values? 3) What group or tribe do you most want to serve, inspire, and impact? 4) What do you most want to teach and represent in this world?

Day 4: Fill in the blank to create a working title for your course: How to _____ **[get desired outcome]** without _____ **[the usual problem].**

Day 5: Run a 1-2 day survey using social media or your email list on surveymonkey.com. Provide at least five course title choices.

Day 6: Fill in the blanks for more clarity: My course _____ _____ **[1. Working title of course]** helps

_____ [2. Tribe or group you most want to impact and work with] learn how to _____ [3. what you are going to teach specifically] so they can _____ [4. the result they will get; what they will be, do, or have after completing your course].

Day 7: What is your BIG promise for students who purchase your online course?

Day 8: Define your avatar by answering some of these questions (interview someone or think of a real person you know who would be your ideal client): Gender; Age; Income Status; Education Status; Family Status; Experience level about your topic (newbie, intermediate, advanced); What type of work do they do?; Hobbies?; What kind of books do they read?; Do they have a spiritual practice?; Where are they feeling most challenged in their lives right now?; What keeps them awake at night (related to your topic)?; What is most important to them right now?; What are their hopes, dreams and aspirations?

Day 9: Write a letter to your ideal client acknowledging their problems, pain, and fears, and explain how your course is the solution to their problems and why you created it. Speak from the heart.

Day 10: Write down three types of people your course is NOT for.

Days 11-14: Validate before you create using these four methods:

METHOD 1: Find courses similar to what you want to create. Check online platforms like: udemy.com, masterclass.com, Lynda.com, or Google your topic with the words "online course." Write down the title, the length of the course, the cost, and list the main benefits. This is your market research.

METHOD 2: Send an email to your list to share that you have a brand new "BETA" program coming out soon called [Working

Title of Course]. Include a link to a landing page where they can sign up to receive more information (more about landing pages below). I use Aweber to collect email addresses for my business (you can use ActiveCampaign, Mailchimp, etc.). You don't need thousands of people to sign up — 25-100 people indicates there is good initial interest.

METHOD 3: Send people from your social media platforms to a landing page to sign up and receive more information about your upcoming program.

METHOD 4: Come up with 4-8 titles around the same topic or niche and create a survey using surveymonkey.com so people can vote on the title. I discovered people loved the title: *"Make Money While You Sleep"* by conducting a survey. I had other good titles, but that got the most votes!

Day 15: Once your course is validated and you've selected your working title, create a course outline using the Mind Dump method. Get a poster board or whiteboard, a pack of Post-it Notes, and a pen. Start thinking of everything you want to teach on your selected topic. Write down one idea/topic on each Post-It Note. Then, arrange similar notes into groups that will become your Module/Lesson topics. Review the notes and remove anything that seems redundant. Reword if needed. Once you're happy with your groupings, transfer them to the course template (see Chapter 4).

Day 16: Using your course outline, create PowerPoint or Keynote slides for each module/lesson.

Day 17: Review the Rapid Writing Secrets and use those when creating course content. Most courses are videos with some handouts. You can write the content on the speaker notes section at the bottom of your slides so you can follow as you record.

Days 18-21: Sign up for Thinkific (you can start with the free program) and create at least two Modules with Lessons for your course. Use your slides to record your content. Create handouts if you like, but don't get stuck on that yet.

Day 22: Have graphics made for your course on fiverr or somewhere with fast turn-around. You can create graphics in Canva if you are proficient in that program. Use the graphics for your Facebook group (public) banner and for the thumbnail on your video lessons. Invite people to join your new Facebook group.

Day 23: Decide on low-ticket or high-ticket. Review Chapter 7 for pros and cons of each. Low-ticket is a DIY course that doesn't require much, if any, of your time. High-ticket requires you to sell from a strategy session/call.

Day 24: Write a sales page for your course using the template in Chapter 6 if you are selling low-ticket. If you are selling high-ticket, you don't need a sales page. Prospects will apply for your program, and you'll do strategy calls to enroll them. You can read my book **Work from Home & Make 6-Figures** which goes over high ticket selling in great detail.

Day 25: Decide which three bonuses you will offer to people who sign up for your course by a certain date.

Day 26: Start finding your MVP's – Most Valuable Payers using the 10 Organic Ways to Get Clients in Chapter 8. Post on multiple platforms daily. If you have an email list, market your BETA program to your email list.

Day 27: Start Selling Your Course using your email list and/or social media platforms.

Day 28-30: Implement at least three ways to sell your course: 5-day free challenge in your Facebook group; Facebook live trainings on your topic where you invite members into your program during the training; offer free tools via a free module with lessons that are part of your full online course on Thinkific as a teaser to get them interested; speak about your topic at virtual summits; use another person's email list and social media to promote your course to and offer a share of the profits.

Please use this blueprint and treat it like it is GOLD!

I wish I had this blueprint when I created my first online course. That was a long time ago, and we didn't have the technology we have today to quickly create, set up, and launch a course.

You purchased this book not to just be *inspired,* but to create a long-term business asset that can make you money and give you more FREEDOM.

If you already have a high-ticket program, a service-based business, or you're just starting out, creating a signature online course will leverage your time and multiply your profits.

Go forth and multiply!

Closing Thoughts

You have a wealth of knowledge to share with the world.

I know it is scary to put yourself out there for fear others will criticize you. Those people usually aren't the ones out there doing the work.

I've always loved this quote by Theodore Roosevelt, and I think it will inspire you as well:

"It is not the critic who counts; not the man who points out how the strong man stumbles, or where the doer of deeds could have done them better. The credit belongs to the man who is actually in the arena, whose face is marred by dust and sweat and blood; who strives valiantly; who errs, who comes short again and again, because there is no effort without error and shortcoming; but who does actually strive to do the deeds; who knows great enthusiasms, the great devotions; who spends himself in a worthy cause; who at the best knows in the end the triumph of high achievement, and who at the worst, if he fails, at least fails while daring greatly, so that his place shall never be with those cold and timid souls who neither know victory nor defeat."

I encourage you to read this quote every day for the next 30 days while you create your online course.

Don't let the fear of criticism or the addiction to approval stop you from living your dreams.

I have failed many times with different programs and books, but that hasn't stopped me. I'm living my dreams now because I've developed a thick skin to the naysayers who give me non-constructive criticism.

Over the years, I've learned that it's easier to sit on the sidelines and criticize than to get in the arena and create something.

I love reading books and often read two books per week. There are some books that I just don't connect with, but I would never consider writing a bad review online about the book or the author. I appreciate all the "creators" who strive to do the deeds.

You have what it takes to be a creator. Take the years of knowledge, wisdom, experience and the mistakes you've made, and teach others.

Go forth and create!

About the Author

MICHELLE KULP is the #1 Amazon best-selling author of *QUIT YOUR JOB & FOLLOW YOUR DREAMS* and *I LOVE MYSELF WHEN...* among others. She lives in small cozy cottage on the Chesapeake Bay in Maryland. Michelle loves inspiring, motivating and educating Author-Preneurs to succeed and live the life of their dreams.

Learn more about Michelle at:
https://www.amazon.com/Michelle-Kulp/e/B006D4EQIY/

Learn more about Michelle's Amazon Bestseller Program at:
www.bestsellingauthorprogram.com

Can You Do Me A Favor?

If you enjoyed this book or found it useful, I'd be very grateful if you'd post a short review on Amazon. Your support really does make a difference, and I read all the reviews personally to get your feedback and make this book even better.

Thanks again for your support!

Affiliate Disclosure

This book contains affiliate links. If you buy using my links, I get a small commission (at no additional cost to you) so I can write even more books!

Made in the USA
Las Vegas, NV
27 February 2021

18733449R00075